High ^tech way Forward..

HIGH-TECH WAY FORWARD

Sunil Khandbahale

https://sunilkhandbahale.com/

CONTENTS

HIGH-TECH WAY FORWARD

..

Sunil Khandbahale

BLESSINGS

Sadguru Shri. Kisan Maharaj Sakhare

MENTOR

Dr. Vijay Bhatkar Sir

SHARING INSIGHTS..

The diverse articles published in these newspapers have received excellent responses from readers. Many new ideas and perspectives have been brought to light by the readers. Numerous opinions and feedback have been received, whether through phone calls, emails, or letters. Despite the busy lifestyle or oversight, some previously published articles have been revisited, and reading sessions have been organized in schools.

These articles have also been broadcasted on the radio, and some have been shared on social media platforms with friends and colleagues. Many young individuals have found encouragement in these writings, leading them to actively engage in practical work based on their ideas. As a result, the overall literary and intellectual atmosphere has become enriching.

I express my sincere gratitude to the editors, journalists, and readers who have collaborated in the various educational programs related to technology via different publishing medias. The compilation of selected articles into a book is a response to the requests and encouragement from many readers, colleagues, friends, and family.

PREFACE

High-Tech Way Forward

Futuristic Innovation Technology

Just imagine that your home is not just on land but also in the sea and in the sky. Self-driving cars, without driver are not only move on roads but also fly in the sky. Your personal, intimate space is not just on the computer screen but projected on any material or even on empty space, and it may not be so far-fetched that you can expect a healthy life for thousands of years. Does it sound like exaggeration? But when it comes directly in the near future, it shouldn't be surprising. Because all over the world, scientists are constantly achieving success in one or more experiments. The current era is different from the era of information. The production of 2.5 quintillion bytes of data occurs every day. The data being generated every day is so vast that 90% of the data in the world has been created only in the past decade. Thanks to the impact of big data, research has accelerated, helping us get closer to the goal in no time.

Under the Meta Connectivity program, solar-powered internet planes, followed by instant 3D-printed medicine capsules placed on the tongue to stop bleeding within just 12 seconds during a serious accident or warfare, are now a reality. In addition, 3D-printed medicine capsules, placed on the tongue, instantly dissolve, preventing blood flow of 3,000 liters in 1 minute during flood conditions, cement that absorbs human urine to produce clean water and energy generation, and research to change the necessary genes in DNA have been successful, allowing new codes to be created in place of codes that do not exist in the genome. The development of Ebola disease prevention vaccines, disease prevention drugs, and planes that will change in the car are now the subject of everyone's discussion, with research on computer manufacturing at just ₹500.

The advent of the Internet of Things has connected billions of devices to each other. In the coming times, the world will be based on information and will be interdependent. Similarly, in the field of medicine, agriculture, architecture, and drug manufacturing, significant progress can be made by installing nanosensors in building materials, similar to the human body. It is now possible to produce inexhaustible energy through batteries based on sodium, zinc, and aluminum, ensuring environmental sustainability, clean, and 24-hour guaranteed electricity. Autonomous vehicles, i.e., self-driving cars, have taken strides in many companies, thus preventing possible loss of life in accidents, pollution reduction, and making the lives of the elderly and differently-abled individuals more enjoyable. The use of Wi-Fi through visible light and long-distance communication through sound waves will make it possible to electrify our internet and electronic devices. In the future, when buildings, roads, and cars start communicating with us on a human scale, it will not be surprising. Robots will teach robots, and in order to be liberated from air pollution, personal air purification devices that attach to the body, organic-on-chip, and a sensor-free thermometer will be created.

The increasing urbanization is a global challenge. Cities become inconvenient due to the congestion of people, animals, waste, buildings, and vehicles, as well as the lack of resources. The definite answer to this is technology. Now there is a strong emphasis on using technology for the planned use of technology globally to make urban life comfortable. In order to make cities smart, the use of technology has become crucial all over the world, as well as awareness among citizens about new technologies is equally important. In this regard, I am grateful to leading dailies like Maharashtra Times, Loksatta, Divya Marathi, Lokmat and Sakal newspaper, for giving me the opportunity to write about technology. I had the opportunity to experience firsthand the changes in technology during the last one and a half years of living in the United States and facing technology like Meta, Google, and IT. The government policies of Western countries, the mindset of their citizens, well-educated human resources, basic infrastructure, and up-to-date resources all contribute to their development, and the practice of all this is useful for their development. It is possible for you too, with efforts, to achieve this easily. In my opinion, the second name of 'problem' is 'opportunity'!

OPEN-DATA INITIATIVE

*Navigating Challenges in
Developing Countries Through
Transparent Information Access*

Oops, there is no water in the tap, and people are running late for their railway-scheduled times, suddenly the city's transportation route changed, and there is an urgent need for blood, but the blood banks don't have the required type of the blood. For the sake of emergency surgeries, there has been a prolonged power outage, and today the office is closed. The authority officer is on leave, and there is no cash in the bank. These are not just one or two instances, but many such situations are not new to us in a country as vast and diverse as India or in many other developing countries. We may understand some challenges that our fellow citizens face, but dealing with crises where no prior information is available can be extremely distressing.

If accurate information about the scheduled events in our city, as well as the availability of resources, is accessible, it could have helped improve the quality of life for citizens. In Western countries, citizens can plan every second of their day. It is possible because they have access to fundamental information through initiatives like 'Open Data Initiative.'

'Open Data' or 'Open Fundamental Information' refers to information that is regularly published on authorized platforms by governmental, non-governmental, and service-oriented organizations. The main goal of 'Open Data' is to enhance the optimal use of national resources, economic development, the status of public services, transparency, and improvement of economic values along with building government responsibility through the means of public engagement and interaction between citizens and the administration. The initiative is known as the 'Open Data Initiative.'

The term 'Open Data' or 'Open Fundamental Information' refers to information that is regularly published on authorized platforms by governmental, non-governmental, and service-oriented organizations. The information is published on a regular basis and is made public without any restriction for the greater good. The main goal of 'Open Data' is to enhance the optimal use of national resources, economic development, the status of public services, transparency, and improvement of economic values along with building government responsibility through the means of public engagement and interaction between citizens and the administration. The initiative is known as the 'Open Data Initiative.'

The benefits of 'Open Data' or 'Open Fundamental Information' are not only limited to institutions and citizens. The concept of 'Deep Data Learning' involves practicing the effective use of information for the creation of new and beneficial plans. The success of various open-source initiatives like 'Open Data' in various countries has been recognized globally.

The Government of India, through the official website data.gov.in, has made available information from approximately 103 departments, comprising more than fifty thousand resources covering over four thousand subjects. This information has become a valuable resource for many young entrepreneurs in the country who are starting their own startups based on the available data.

In the era of social media and information technology, the importance of the 'Wisdom of Crowds' is widely understood. The 'Wisdom of Crowds' refers to the collective knowledge of people in solving complex problems, where an individual, organization, or community works towards finding effective solutions rather than relying on personal efforts. Many successful examples of crowd-sourced initiatives, such as Waze for traffic information, Google

Maps for navigation, Wikipedia as a free and open encyclopedia, Linux for operating systems, Mozilla Firefox web browser, Lego for popular games, and Airbnb and Uber for successful crowd-sourced solutions, have had a significant impact. This approach has proven effective in addressing global issues and is being adopted by many countries.

In the changing environment, rising temperatures, education, and health, inequality, poverty, increasing corruption, and unemployment are global challenges for which many countries are sharing their information and statistics for the public good. The United Nations, through initiatives like the 'Open Data' and the 'Wisdom of Crowds,' is actively promoting global human skill development by implementing awareness and education programs on a large scale. In addition to this, companies like Google and Meta are also contributing to empowering the new generation with their technological knowledge through the means of 'Open Data' for creating new employment opportunities.

In the process of building a Smart City, the involvement of citizens is of paramount importance. With the enthusiastic participation of citizens, through the means of 'Open Data,' we can contribute comprehensively to the development of our city. Efforts towards creating innovative plans with the help of the youth in the city can be fruitful. Digitizing various civic amenities through e-governance, as well as keeping local administration up-to-date with public information, appears to be promising.

DECODING SMART CITIES

A Comprehensive Exploration of Smart Technologies and Their Impact on Urban Living.

S mart City! What does it take to make a city smart, and what needs to be done? By whom? What are the benefits, and for whom? These are common questions that both you and I, the general public, have.

Indeed, the concept of a Smart City is not a universally defined one. It is determined by the collective aspirations, needs, available resources, power, security, and adherence to standards of the local citizens and administration. Therefore, mimicking the success of smart cities in developed nations is not possible, nor is it universally applicable. Another interpretation is that the decision to make your city smart is entirely up to you. Despite this, a general understanding of the concept of Smart Cities has emerged. According to this understanding, a Smart City is one that uses modern information technology and internet-based (Internet of Things) services to enhance the quality of life, elevate the standard of living of local citizens, and address issues such as water supply, power supply, healthcare, waste management, efficient transportation, economic considerations for the average person, internet connectivity, e-governance, universal education, cleanliness, and security.

Under the Indian government's 'Smart City Mission,' comprehensive development guidelines have been provided for smart cities, encompassing physical, social, and economic infrastructure. These guidelines aim to create smart environments within cities, including new, well-planned smart neighborhoods. The plan is to integrate essential services such as continuous water supply, efficient power supply, healthcare, waste management, functional transportation systems, and technology-driven governance, education, cleanliness, and security into the fabric of the city.

In 2016, the Indian government selected 97 cities under the Smart City Mission. This brings us to the topic of smart technologies. However, making cities truly smart is facilitated by smart technologies. As seen in the past, creating new, locally useful technologies from information publicly available, known as 'open data,' is vital. In this regard, the development of smart technologies by local technologists through crowd-sourcing information and creating innovative solutions is essential for the success of smart cities. In the following articles, we will explore examples of such smart technologies developed through 'open data' that are particularly useful in every smart city.

1. Smart Parking System

An American friend searching for Indian restaurants around Boston Common used the Google search term 'Indian restaurants around Boston Common' on his mobile. After seeing the available options, he opened a smart parking app on his phone, checking where parking spots were available. Having found a spot, he made it right away. In cases where parking was not available for the next hour, he decided to abandon the car and walk a little further, which turned out to be more convenient for us. In foreign countries, well-designed parking systems in tall, multifunctional buildings offer efficient and significantly reduced parking space. By developing smart parking systems and apps through local crowd-sourcing, significant fuel savings and reduced mental stress during travel are achievable.

2. Public Touchscreens

While wandering around the city of Chicago in the United States, I came across public places and many intersections with touchscreens installed. I later learned that this was a joint venture between the Chicago administration and a company called 'Elevate Digital.' These touchscreen kiosks, strategically placed on various intersections, attract attention. Using more than 120 interactive applications, citizens can obtain public information, read advertisements to get discounts, and even make purchases at favorable rates. The touchscreen facility allows citizens to change the conversation on public roads significantly. Through this, the government can accumulate data on citizens' habits, helping them predict changes through predictive analysis. Further advancements in facial recognition and gesture interfaces are also being attempted through touchscreen interfaces.

These are just a couple of examples of how smart technologies, when integrated into city life, can contribute to making cities smarter, more efficient, and more comfortable for their residents.

CONNECTIVITY REVOLUTION

Unveiling the Potential of Municipal Wireless Networks in the Era of 'Wi-Fi City'.

I n the preceding article, we have understood the concept of a smart city in the previous lesson, and we have also learned about various initiatives happening globally based on 'open data' from local administration and public participation in the process of making cities smart, especially focusing on smart parking and public touchscreens. In the current lesson, we will gather information on the topic of 'Wi-Fi City,' meaning 'Municipal Wireless Network.'

In the municipal areas, providing free internet access to citizens by building wireless internet networks at public places is referred to as 'Municipal Wireless Network.' In the United States and some other countries, I have not felt the need for it while traveling because there is open Wi-Fi internet available everywhere, including subways, railway stations, bus stops, moving vehicles, libraries, pharmacies, universities, and at every corner of the city. The whole city seems to be covered with Wi-Fi. Citizens prefer to eat in restaurants with free internet, and young people in the virtual world can be seen crowded at Starbucks for coffee and McDonald's for pizza-burgers. One reason for this is the availability of free Wi-Fi internet there.

The provision of free Wi-Fi internet has become a successful business strategy for brands like Starbucks and McDonald's. The availability of free internet services has led to a significant increase in the revenue of many businesses. According to a recent survey, 62% of businesses said that customers spend more time in areas with Wi-Fi zones, and 50% said that customers spend more money since they started providing free internet services. Attracting more customers, assessing the value-added services, and generating significant business profits through facilities like Wi-Fi have become smart business strategies.

The serious consideration of 'Municipal Wireless Network' is evident from the fact that governments of many countries, including India, have started thinking about it seriously. The spread of Wi-Fi networks throughout the city leads to increased usage of government services, improved public transportation systems, new employment opportunities, increased innovation, growth in tourism business, enhanced public engagement, and the creation of new assets for municipalities through advertisements and data. The impact of free education through the dissemination of information has reduced the digital divide.

During an emergency situation caused by a storm in the state of Vermont in the United States, the entire communication system in the Royalton city had collapsed. At such a crisis, citizens quickly took advantage of the Wi-Fi internet provided by the administration for immediate contact. By establishing internet kiosks in small departments, they were able to start the limited internet service within 24 hours, providing immediate information through various networks in times of crisis. By controlling the local Wi-Fi network, the landing page of the main signaling site (landing page) can be set, which helps in providing immediate information to citizens through networks related to that network during emergencies. The landing page can provide information such as emergency information in the city, places of importance, architecture, museums, public viewing places, city events, traffic rates and schedules, banks and ATMs, pharmacies, schools and colleges, marketplaces, nearby malls, theaters, and other important information or entertainment events through advertising and data. Providing direct visible information to local citizens and tourists through the local Wi-

Fi network is not only a delightful experience but also contributes to the intellectual, social, and economic development of the urban community as a whole. Maximum information is essential for the all-around development of the city. At such times, analyzing the available data through Municipal Wireless Internet and creating plans for the welfare of citizens will be helpful. Many cities attract attention nationally and internationally by showcasing their unique features through Wi-Fi-City branding.

Now, along with "food, clothing, and shelter," mobile and internet have also become basic needs of human civilization. In cities like Los Angeles, Canada, Taiwan, Paris, and many others, successful use of free internet is underway in every government building, public transportation, and tourist locations. Cities affected by smart cities in progressive nations, such as Bangalore, Delhi, Kolkata, and Ahmedabad in India, are making limited efforts to establish Municipal Wireless Networks. In the age of information technology, connectivity, especially high-speed internet connectivity, plays a crucial role alongside highways. In the United States, approximately 85% of the population uses the internet, and about 70% of people have access to high-speed internet all the time. India has 127th place in internet usage, with about 26% of Indians using the internet. The concept of limited internet includes 3G, 4G, and internet expenses that are not affordable for everyone. However, the fact that there are more than one billion smartphones in the country is a positive aspect for India. If free and secure internet is available, it will lead to significant savings for the general public, and, in turn, many employment opportunities will be available. Students and entrepreneurs can benefit more. Uninterrupted (non-intercepted) internet and its speed play a crucial role in the continuous process of distance learning. In the Digital India process, efforts are being made to consider new possibilities, and demand for practical information is increasing. Imagining that as part of the welfare program, providing secure and free internet across the country will be beneficial.

TECH-DRIVEN GENEROSITY

*Navigating the Sharing Economy
in the tech era.*

While navigating smart city technologies, we have learned about the 'Municipal Wireless Network,' which is synonymous with the concept of 'Wi-Fi City.' In the current text, discussions revolve around how cities are becoming self-sufficient through the 'Sharing Economy' or 'Collaborative Economy' and how technology plays a role in these processes.

I once visited a friend in Chicago. A vehicle from a social organization came to his place. Taking various items, including furniture and a TV, from the side of the road to be kept at home, made me ponder. That's when I learned about Jhils Good, a technology company based in Chicago. This organization facilitates the donation of your items for social causes, creating an excellent platform for interaction between donors and recipients. The donated items, such as household appliances, children's clothes and toys, books and magazines, cameras and radios, phones and computers, printers, clotheslines, food, and more, are easily distributed through the organization's website. Individuals can register to donate items, and those in need can register to receive them. Urgent needs, organization details, and donation requirements are published on the platform, making it easy for people to find the necessary items. The choice of items to donate and whether to deliver them to the organization or have them picked up from your home is entirely at the discretion of the donor. The organization facilitates dialogue between both parties, ensuring mutual agreement. After this simple process, the donated items find a new home. This not only prevents items from going to waste but also allows people to fulfill their needs at minimal cost.

Many times, we are faced with the question of what to do with items we no longer need. To address this, we often postpone it, thinking it will come in handy someday. This clutter accumulates even at home. While it is good to donate, to whom? There is no shortage of needs in society. Where should one look for someone in need? It takes a considerable amount of time. Eventually, some items end up in the trash, causing waste. Despite having the intention to donate, the thought of dismantling items in good condition into scrap becomes disheartening. Even for someone in need, the challenge lies in finding a specific item among the vast array of available products. Occasionally, items with sentimental value are among the donated ones, making the process emotional.

Sometimes, items that were not being used at all, such as a car whose battery was dead, tires that were damaged, a dress that went out of style, or goods going to waste because there was no internet at home, could be valuable for others. Rather than purchasing new items, sharing them through a 'sharing economy' could be more sustainable. If everyone shared each item instead of buying new ones every time, it would lead to a more sustainable and affordable lifestyle. Sharing economy, meaning collaborative economy, refers to an economic system where citizens can provide each other with public assets and services either free or at a low cost, fostering mutual cooperation.

The Silicon Valley-based American friends had come to India for two weeks. They had rented their home through Airbnb. Instead of paying for parking at the airport, they chose to use the services of a taxi company called Zipcar. In progressive nations, many citizens are willing to share their belongings with others without the need for personal ownership, thanks to the process of technology embedded in the sharing economy or collaborative economy.

While in Chicago, I visited a friend. A social organization's van arrived at their place, and they donated various items from their home, including furniture and electronics, to be used by those in need. I inquired about this, and that led me to understand how technology is inspiring cities to take up the concept of the sharing economy or collaborative economy in their processes.

In the sharing economy, individuals take items that are surplus in their homes to the organization, which facilitates easy distribution of various new and old items, such as household appliances, children's clothes, books, magazines, cameras, radios, phones, printers, clothing, and more. People can decide what items they want to donate and register them with the organization. The needs of individuals, the organization, and their respective requirements are published on the organization's platform. Available items, both new and old, are easily accessible, contributing to a seamless exchange process.

Often, there is a dilemma about what to do with items that are not needed. Sometimes, they end up unused at home, causing clutter. However, by donating such items to the organization, they find a new home, and the process becomes more organized. The organization's website provides information about household items, children's clothes and toys, books and magazines, cameras and radios, phones and computers, printers, gardening tools, and various other new and old items. The organization's platform facilitates easy exchange of these items. Individuals can register what they want to donate and what they need from the organization. The needs of individuals, the organization, and their respective requirements are published on the organization's platform.

A crucial aspect of this process is that individuals have complete freedom to decide what they want to donate and can access these items from the organization to use at home or donate them to someone else. The needs and preferences of individuals, the organization, and the needs of those who use these items are published on the organization's platform. The organization provides information about the items available, and individuals can register what they need. The organization acts as a mediator and facilitates the easy exchange of items, allowing the participants to communicate and agree upon the terms. The available items can be easily accessed, ensuring a smooth process.

In this way, the organization becomes a hub for facilitating the sharing economy, and individuals can actively participate in the process of donating and receiving items. The organization encourages individuals, the organization, and those in need to interact, creating a vibrant platform for sharing resources.

The concept of the sharing economy is not limited to physical items but extends to services as well. In Chicago, I learned about the Good Grid, a technology company dedicated to social work. They encourage people to donate their items for social causes and facilitate meetings between donors and recipients through their platform. Soon, they were going to move to a new home, and they had donated items that they no longer needed through this organization. The organization provides easy access to household items, children's clothing, books, and magazines, cameras, radios, phones, printers, gardening tools, and various new and old items.

Individuals can decide what items they want to donate and register them with the organization. The organization's platform provides information about available items, and people can easily access these items to meet their needs. Whether you want to make a donation or receive items from the organization, individuals can register and participate in the process. The needs and preferences of individuals, the organization, and those in need are published on the organization's platform.

The organization encourages individuals, the organization, and those in need to interact, creating a vibrant platform for sharing resources. The organization facilitates dialogue between donors and recipients, and mutual agreement is reached through discussion. The process is transparent and leads to a harmonious exchange of goods. The open discussion about this straightforward process has shed light on the significant contribution of technology to the sharing economy.

Sometimes, you may wonder what to do with items that are not needed. Eventually, it leads to contemplation, and over time, you may find a solution. While the car was unusable due to a dead battery, a flat tire, or it being stolen, they had installed a solar-powered fence around their home. The items that were no longer useful to them were donated through this organization. The organization provides easy access to various new and old items, such as household items, children's clothing, books, magazines, cameras, radios, phones, printers, gardening tools, and more. Individuals can easily access these items and meet their needs.

Individuals can decide what items they want to donate and register them with the organization. The organization's platform provides information about available items, and people can easily access these items to meet their needs. Whether you want to make a donation or receive items from the organization, individuals can register and participate in the process. The needs and preferences of individuals, the organization, and those in need are published on the organization's platform.

The organization facilitates dialogue between donors and recipients, and mutual agreement is reached through discussion. The process is transparent and leads to a harmonious exchange of goods. The open discussion about this straightforward process has shed light on the significant contribution of technology to the sharing economy.

Often, there is a dilemma about what to do with items that are not needed. Sometimes, they end up unused at home, causing clutter. However, by donating such items to the organization, they find a new home, and the process becomes more organized. The organization's website provides information about household items, children's clothes and toys, books and magazines, cameras and radios, phones and computers, printers, gardening tools, and various other new and old items. The organization's platform facilitates easy exchange of these items. Individuals can register what they want to donate and what they need from the organization. The needs of individuals, the organization, and their respective requirements are published on the organization's platform. A crucial aspect of this process is that individuals have complete freedom.

PEDALING PROGRESS

*Exploring the Urban Landscape
Through Bike Sharing.*

On the night of May 4, 2014, I reached Washington, D.C. The capital of America looked enchanting in the glow of lights. I had some knowledge about the city from my studies, but this was my first direct encounter. The second day turned out to be even more interesting for me. After exploring the nearby areas, I decided to plan my visit with a rented bicycle.

I started my day early in the morning. Riding towards Wisconsin Avenue Northwest, I noticed a well-marked lane for bicycles. Intrigued, I investigated further and discovered the "Capital Bikeshare" program, which had stations spread across the city. There were around forty-four such stations with four thousand bicycles in operation. They could be rented for as little as two dollars for thirty minutes and eight dollars for a full day. I decided to rent a bicycle for eight dollars.

I downloaded the Capital Bikeshare app on my mobile and headed towards the National Mall. Every half a kilometer to a kilometer, I spotted Capital Bikeshare stations. At each location, I docked my bike, explored the surrounding areas, and consulted the station map on my mobile in case I got lost. This routine continued throughout the day. By the end of the day, I had covered approximately fifteen to twenty kilometers, exploring various parts of the city. It was a unique joy to experience the city up close and personal.

Despite spending just eight dollars, I felt the true value of the Capital Bikeshare program. I continued to use it out of love for bike-sharing. I also experienced bike-sharing in cities like New York, the Bay Area, Portland, and Chicago. In the following year, as I attended MIT, my first job in Boston was with the "Hubway" bike-sharing program. I used bicycles for daily commuting for about a year, saving money and contributing to reducing traffic and pollution.

Beyond economic benefits, regular cycling kept me healthy, and the time saved from avoiding traffic contributed to a more productive day. It allowed me to affordably travel between America and India for two years. Besides financial gains, the bike-sharing experience in Boston, Cambridge, and neighboring areas was enriching.

Bike-sharing refers to a service that provides bicycles for short-term personal use. Throughout the city, bicycle stands are spread, and citizens can become members monthly or annually. Tourists can also use the service as temporary members. Specially designed bikes, theft-proof and low-maintenance, are provided, and users can access any bike at any time using a card or password. Bike-sharing not only reduces the cost of parking and vehicle maintenance but also encourages people to choose cycling over other modes of transportation.

In Europe, Amsterdam started an innovative bike-sharing program in 1965, which has since spread to fifty countries and over seven hundred cities. With forty thousand bike stations and nearly nine million bicycles, bike-sharing has become a popular alternative for public transportation. Due to the availability of bike-sharing networks in prominent locations within cities, members receive numerous benefits and discounts.

To encourage more citizens to use bike-sharing, some organizations, along with parks, museums, corporations, bus services, railways, airports, and car companies, participate in the initiative. Initiatives like "Bike to Work" and "Bike to School" promote cycling culture. Entrepreneurs and special organizations actively collaborate with bike-sharing networks as part of their business strategy. Paris's Velib, Washington's Capital Bikeshare, Boston's Hubway, Los Angeles's Metro Bike, New York's Citi Bike,

Minneapolis's Nice Ride, Montreal's Bixi, Berlin's Call a Bike, and Japan's EcoBike are examples of companies successfully running such programs.

The success of bike-sharing businesses is largely attributed to "Big Data." Each bike in the network is equipped with an RFID sensor. This sensor collects data on the bike's origin, destination, and complete journey, providing comprehensive information on every trip. This data, processed through information technology, is crucial for planning future services, urban administration, and civic planning to ensure the development of services and products according to citizens' needs. By leveraging technology, bike-sharing networks send real-time data on bike usage, routes, and other vital information.

The wireless service for bicycles plays a significant role in collecting and transmitting data. Through the use of RFIDs, members can access real-time information about bike availability, routes, and other relevant details. This efficient use of technology allows companies to plan future services based on concrete data. It also facilitates the administration of local government, enabling them to plan and implement policies that are beneficial for urban management and citizens.

The growth of bike-sharing businesses can be attributed to the innovative use of "Big Data." The widespread deployment of sensors on bikes, coupled with advanced data processing technology, enables the collection of valuable information. This data is essential for planning future services and urban development. The success of bike-sharing networks reflects not only financial gains but also the positive impact on the environment, health, and overall urban lifestyle.

In our cities, public transportation is already under pressure. Schools and colleges have lakhs of students, and working-class individuals commute every day. People from rural areas come to cities for employment, and thousands of tourists visit throughout the year. The increasing air pollution, fuel shortages, growing population, and their demands put significant stress on transportation systems. However, in progressive nations, cycling has been an important mode of transportation from the beginning.

Even in the face of challenges such as road accidents, non-availability of dedicated cycling lanes, and security concerns, there is a growing trend of people choosing bicycles for commuting. If the government provides basic infrastructure and adopts appropriate policies, the number of cyclists is sure to increase. The awareness about citizens' health is also increasing. Citizens are becoming more conscious of their changing habits, their future, the need for alternative transportation, and are considering local entrepreneurs for cycling sharing.

With the changing preferences of citizens, their habits, the need for alternative transportation, and local entrepreneurs' potential contribution, cycling sharing is emerging as a viable business opportunity. For local youth, this can generate significant employment opportunities. Collaboration with local businesses, industrial organizations, and transportation authorities can also be explored. In addition to traditional means of transportation, cycling sharing schemes can provide an alternative means of local transportation.

Apart from being an eco-friendly and healthy mode of transportation, cycling sharing can contribute to the local economy. It aligns with the changing preferences of citizens, their future, the demand for transportation alternatives, and local entrepreneurs' needs. Creating attractive and safe cycling routes, along with using technology for efficient sharing systems, can lead to effective transportation management. Collaborative efforts with technological solutions can make cycling sharing schemes as effective contributors to transportation systems.

As smart cities adopt cycling sharing as an environmentally friendly and health-promoting alternative, it is poised to make a significant impact.

EMPOWERING URBAN FUTURES

Harnessing Community Solar Systems for Sustainable Cities

While implementing smart cities, we have gathered information on various crucial aspects such as governance, transportation, waste management, economy, environment, and information and technology. In the current context, let's explore the concept of 'Community Solar Systems' while delving into the importance of energy in this chapter.

Imagine if public spaces in the city, such as parks, playgrounds, open spaces, roads, water reservoirs, canals, rivers, and dams, were equipped with elevated solar panels. This could result in cooling of parks and playgrounds, fresh air along the roads, and conservation of water sources from the sunlight. What if, in addition to these benefits, electricity could also be generated for household use? According to the principles of renewable energy, total energy in the world is constant and stable. It cannot be lost; it can only be transformed from one form to another. Therefore, with the growing population and urbanization, there is a need to explore new ways to reduce our dependence on traditional energy sources.

Sun has been the primary source of energy since time immemorial. While other sources of energy are finite, the effective use of solar technology has made the production of solar energy successful. However, solar energy is still underutilized due to its intermittent nature and high initial costs, especially in urban areas where space is limited and conflicts with existing structures are common. This is where the concept of 'Community Solar Systems' or community solar gardens/farms comes into play. These are solar energy facilities built cooperatively by communities, often providing more homes with energy than individually constructed or commercially available solar installations. It is crucial for these projects to be community-owned, allowing people to have a stake in the initiative. The size of the project can vary from a small installation on a rooftop to a larger, fully commercialized solar farm.

The use of virtual net metering enables individuals in the community to benefit from the total energy generated by the project. Community solar has gained popularity globally, offering a new business opportunity in the emerging virtual world. With advancements in information and technology, human society is actively working towards generating energy for both individual and collective use in an environmentally friendly and controlled manner (Customized and Controlled Energy Consumption).

The Mojave name company located in the United States provides facilities for investing in community solar projects. To promote the use of solar energy in communities, governments worldwide, including in Florida, have been encouraging citizens to participate in solar projects through various incentives. In Denver, Colorado, Kitson and partner companies collaborated in 2006 with the U.S. government, environmental and IBM technology companies to establish the Babcock Ranch, the first updated community solar project in the United States, spanning over a thousand acres. This project aims to provide solar energy in the form of renewable energy to a population of around fifty thousand people, contributing to environmental technologies in the newly established city.

Various companies in the United States, such as VUI-Sun-Alliance, Microgrid, and Clean-Coalitions in Connecticut, Massachusetts, New Jersey, and Pennsylvania, are actively working to reduce carbon emissions and promote renewable energy production. Examples of successful community solar energy projects include Maryland's University Park

Community Solar Project, Colorado's Clean Energy Collective, Washington's Benbrige Island's Sakai Solar, California's SolarShare, Florida's Orlando Utilities Commission, Vermont, and Utah's solar projects.

As of today, around fifty percent of the global population resides in cities, and this percentage is expected to rise to seventy-five percent by the year 2050. While seventy-five percent of total energy consumption is attributed to cities, carbon dioxide emissions occur mainly within urban areas. Therefore, environmental considerations have become central to urban planning. Due to the high energy consumption of buildings and transportation systems, there is a growing emphasis on integrating smart grids and centralized urban energy management. Signals, vehicles, and wherever possible, transportation systems are incorporating the use of solar energy in these smart grid systems.

In India, construction of fifty percent new buildings in urban areas is expected to take place by the year 2040. Hence, there is a significant emphasis on creating infrastructure and facilities that are energy-efficient. The use of renewable energy sources such as solar and wind for cooling, heating, cooking, and appliances in buildings is being promoted for its simplicity. With the involvement of young entrepreneurs and businessmen in the commercial sector, the cost of renewable energy production can be significantly reduced through appropriate technology and research. Effective government policies, along with the practical application of technology, can make cities truly energy-smart.

IOT REALMS

The Internet of Things Revolution in Smart Cities and Beyond

The Walt Disney Company produced movies like 'Toy Story' or 'Cars.' Do you remember a cinema where toys and cars communicate with each other? The Internet of Things (IoT) is a concept where various entities like trees, animals, humans, buildings in cities, roads, air, water, and vehicles can communicate with each other. Sounds fascinating, right? Thanks to the technological revolution, this is now possible. The Internet of Things refers to a system where devices with unique identification (ID), such as machinery and electronic or digital devices, are interconnected via the internet (network) and can exchange real-time information without human intervention. Computer scientist Kevin Ashton first conceptualized the Internet of Things in 1999. According to contemporary computer science, computers had to rely entirely on human-entered data, such as typing, voice, or scanned information. However, the Internet of Things revolutionized this by allowing devices to communicate and provide real-time information without human intervention, making human life more convenient.

In today's world, the Internet of Things is making a significant impact on various industries in many cities. However, going forward, a significant challenge is to integrate the entire system, meaning more components working together to achieve unified communication. For example, information from traffic systems can be used to improve healthcare devices. How traffic information can be utilized in healthcare systems is just one example of the potential synergies between different components of a smart city. The integration of various systems is crucial for achieving holistic results in areas such as transportation, healthcare, environment, services, education, water management, cleanliness, and security.

The Internet of Things is currently being utilized effectively in different cities for various applications. However, the future challenge is to integrate multiple components for more efficient and collaborative communication. For instance, information from transportation systems can be used to enhance healthcare devices, or how environmental services in urban areas can adapt to changes in air quality. The need for collaboration and synergy among different components becomes essential for comprehensive and effective results.

In Manchester, CityVerve has implemented smart bus stops where travelers waiting for a bus receive instant information, and the bus driver is notified immediately if there are passengers waiting. The company Shoothill in Porto transformed the city's waste management system by using sensors on garbage trucks and buses, providing real-time data on waste collection and optimizing routes through the Internet of Moving Things. In Barcelona, a company named Urbiotica uses sensors in parking spaces to create an efficient parking management system. Wireless sensors provide real-time information to drivers, reducing traffic congestion by 10%.

In the realm of sports, the use of IoT is expanding. For example, in Bristol, Cityzen Sensing uses sensors in footballs and tennis rackets to analyze players' performance, helping athletes improve their skills. In Oxford, Flood Network has developed a flood monitoring system using sensors in various locations, providing real-time information to aid in immediate response planning.

The Internet of Things is playing a crucial role in the development of smart cities. It is expected that IoT will bring significant changes to urban life in the future. The integration of IoT in daily life, from human bodies to inanimate objects, is bringing about extraordinary advancements in fields such as healthcare, agriculture, architecture, and pharmaceuticals. With nanosensors installed in living beings and objects, remarkable progress is being made in medical, agricultural, architectural, and pharmaceutical sectors.

The development of smart cities through the Internet of Things is gaining immense importance in today's fast-paced lifestyle. With IoT, cities are becoming more connected and technologically advanced, bringing about a revolution in various industries. As we move forward, the impact of IoT on urban life is expected to be substantial, with the potential for significant economic growth. According to the International Data Corporation (IDC), the IoT market is expected to reach a staggering $1.7 trillion by 2020. This immense market opportunity holds great potential for entrepreneurs and businesses worldwide. In conclusion, the Internet of Things is not just a technological innovation; it is a transformative force that has the power to shape the future of cities and industries around the globe.

GIGANTIC POWER OF BIG DATA

Transforming Governance, Smart Cities, and Industries

In the previous section, we saw that the administration has taken the initiative called 'Open Data Initiative' to make updated information available to citizens. This is part of the 'Administration-Citizen Information Provision' process. On the other side, citizens provide the administration with structured (standardized) and unstructured (non-standardized) information, collectively known as 'Big Data.' In this section, we will learn more about the subject of 'Big Data.'

The term 'Big Data' refers to the massive amount of digital data generated at an extraordinary speed with the help of modern technology. Every day, around 2.5 quintillion bytes of data are created worldwide. Simply put, this is equivalent to creating a new stack of data reaching the height of Mount Everest every two years. Devices such as phones, sensors, social media posts, websites, digital images, videos, print and broadcast media, emails, GPS, and Internet of Things (IoT) devices are the primary sources of Big Data. This wealth of information is crucial for companies to understand how they operate, how purchases are made, how weather patterns are recorded, or how improvements are made. Many experts and powerful computing systems work extensively in the field of data analysis to extract accurate predictions through the processing of Big Data.

Examples of the practical application of Big Data abound. In the United States, efforts are made to predict where crimes might occur within the next 12 hours. In England, businesspeople and scholars reportedly unveil secret earnings through mathematical analysis. In South Africa, an astrophysicist is engrossed in cataloging the entire universe. All these events are interconnected by a common thread, and that thread is 'Big Data.'

If companies like Google, Amazon, and eBay can benefit from Big Data, why not local administrations? Big Data presents a significant opportunity for administrations to learn from citizens' reactions. Social media platforms provide information on citizens' feelings, issues they talk about, discussions they engage in, and what is happening and about to happen, forming a valuable source of feedback. Many administrations around the world hire data scientists to analyze Big Data, allowing for accurate predictions and improving citizen services and law enforcement.

One successful example is Songdo in South Korea, a city making excellent use of Big Data. By integrating the Internet of Things and Big Data, the city effectively addresses issues such as pollution, transportation, water supply, energy, waste, and parking. Similarly, in Nashik, during the Kumbh Mela, the administration used Big Data to manage crowds efficiently and attend to various challenges. In the United States, Los Angeles uses data for controlling tourist crowds, and in Saudi Arabia, Mecca utilizes Big Data to control crowds during the Haj pilgrimage.

The comprehensive overview of 'Big Data' and its potential applications in various sectors like banking, education, healthcare, social and economic development, marketing, and resource management indicates its significant impact. With the continuous growth of urbanization and population, Big Data is becoming even more prominent. Therefore, utilizing Big Data becomes crucial for smart governance and building smart cities.

As we delve deeper into the applications of Big Data, there is a growing demand for professionals in the field of 'Data Mimansa and Management.' Industries such as banking, education, healthcare, and marketing can undergo a revolution by analyzing data generated in their respective sectors. In the health sector, analyzing data can simplify understanding public health issues, lifestyle patterns, and future health-related trends. In social and economic development and service delivery, significant advancements can be achieved by studying and analyzing Big Data. Moreover, by using natural resources wisely, we can address environmental concerns effectively.

The widespread reach and impact of Big Data are immense. Municipalities are beginning to leverage their resources or seek assistance from major IT companies to acquire Big Data and plan for city development. Companies like IBM, Infosys, TCS, and Wipro play a substantial role in the field of Big Data. For instance, Microsoft CityNext has signed an agreement with the Surat Municipal Corporation for Big Data usage.

The continued urbanization and population growth, synonymous with the rise of Big Data, bring forth the importance of smart governance and the need for real-time analysis of historical and current data. Big Data plays a crucial role in building smart cities, and its integration with the Internet of Things forms the backbone of smart governance.

THE SMART HEALTH HORIZON

A Futuristic Journey into Personalized Medicine and Global Healthcare Collaboration

The pictures are not far away now, as futuristic devices (sensors) will interact with your body for health check-ups (scans) and engage in self-dialogue with remote healthcare professionals. Analyzing available data extensively in moments, health experts will suggest a personalized (personalized) prescription and utilize 3D printers to create pills tailored for you. Human intervention beyond significant actions will be maintained by smart health machines 24/7. While sharing personal health information can be sensitive, the evolving era of available health-related big data could benefit humanity as a whole. Therefore, there is a renewed consideration for global cooperation in the healthcare sector, focusing on addressing local as well as global health challenges. Big data, the Internet of Things (IoT), and increasing reliance on technology are positively shaping the approach of health-related companies and governments.

According to the World Health Organization, there is a shortage of 4.3 million doctors worldwide, with India alone lacking six lakh doctors. The increasing global population and the unmet human resource needs in the health sector highlight the significance of mobile health in the future. With the assistance of highly efficient and cost-effective digital sensors, data on various environmental factors such as air quality, cleanliness, temperature, sound, vibration, pressure, water quality, speed, pollution, etc., can be collected. The integration of Artificial Intelligence (AI) and machine learning can analyze the separated big data to identify contaminated water or food sources, contributing to mitigating waterborne or foodborne diseases. The use of drone technology for inspecting water bodies and providing remote disease control is feasible. The use of mobile phone data can track people's movements and help prevent the spread of contagious diseases, acting as an early warning system. Local administrations gather medical information for public awareness and crisis management.

To create awareness about health issues, medical information is made public, enabling citizens to stay informed, aiding in preparedness for potential crises, and facilitating compliance with laws and regulations. Medical information is made public to build awareness about health issues, aiding in preparedness for potential crises, and facilitating compliance with laws and regulations. In order to promote health, technology such as 3D printing, artificial intelligence, and machine learning are utilized for individualized healthcare plans, making significant strides in the future of healthcare.

The city of San Francisco has initiated the "Heat Vulnerability Index" project to address the impact of climate change, rising temperatures, and the associated risks of diseases and mortality. As a result, the public health department of San Francisco has developed a system for effective communication and collaboration among residents and public health workers by studying satellite images, temperature, and demographics. Oslo, Norway, uses sensors and Skype video for the elderly's care, making healthcare more accessible and cost-effective. Dubai has witnessed a significant increase in medical tourists seeking solutions to health issues, resulting in substantial revenue generated through medical tourism.

Smart cities necessitate a holistic public health approach. This includes the creation of nature-friendly parks, open gyms for exercise, well-maintained sports fields, yoga and meditation centers, cycling paths, car-free zones, aesthetically pleasing public spaces, clean and pure drinking water, proper waste management, and clean public facilities. Simultaneously, the efficient management of chronic diseases, patient registration, telemedicine, remote health monitoring, preventive healthcare, telemedicine, and distance healthcare require collaboration and communication between health experts and healthcare professionals. The collaboration between health data, health analysis, smart cards for patients, gamification, and medical tourism offers significant business opportunities for young entrepreneurs and businesses in the health tourism sector.

TRANSFORMATIVE VIRTUAL REALITY (VR)

A Journey into the Past, Present, and Future of Immersive Technology

In the not-so-distant past, the concept of Virtual Reality (VR) existed mainly in the realm of science fiction. The idea of stepping into a virtual world seemed fantastical, a dream confined to the pages of futuristic novels and blockbuster movies. However, the narrative has drastically shifted, and today, VR is not just a reality; it's a force reshaping the way we perceive, engage, and interact with the world around us. Our journey through the landscape of virtual reality begins with its origins—where the seeds of this immersive technology were first sown, and unfolds to its present state, where VR has found its way into diverse industries, from entertainment to healthcare, education to engineering. Let's see this exploration of a technological odyssey that spans decades, experiencing the evolution of VR from a pioneering idea to a transformative force influencing our daily lives.

Virtual Reality (VR) refers to a computer-generated simulation of an interactive and immersive environment that can be experienced and interacted with by individuals using specialized hardware, such as VR headsets or gloves. In a virtual reality environment, users are often presented with a three-dimensional, computer-generated space that can simulate real-world scenarios or create entirely fantastical worlds. The goal of virtual reality is to provide users with a sense of presence, making them feel as if they are physically present in the simulated environment. This is achieved through the use of various sensory stimuli, including visual, auditory, and, in some cases, haptic feedback. VR applications can span a wide range of fields, including entertainment, education, healthcare, gaming, training, and more, offering users a unique and immersive experience beyond the confines of the physical world.

The roots of Virtual Reality can be traced back to the mid-20th century, a time when the world was on the cusp of technological revolutions. It was during this era that visionaries like Morton Heilig dared to imagine an immersive experience that transcended the limitations of traditional media. Heilig's Sensorama, conceived in the 1950s, was an early attempt at creating a multi-sensory cinematic experience that paved the way for what we now know as virtual reality. Fast forward to the 21st century, and we find ourselves standing on the shoulders of those early pioneers. The journey from Heilig's Sensorama to the sophisticated VR headsets of today has been marked by continuous innovation and relentless pursuit of a more immersive digital experience. As technology advanced, so did our ability to simulate environments that transport users to places only limited by imagination. The advent of computer graphics in the 1980s laid the groundwork for VR as we know it. Devices like the VPL Research DataGlove and the NASA-developed VIEW headset were early attempts at creating interactive virtual spaces. However, it wasn't until the 2010s that VR truly entered the mainstream with the launch of devices like the Oculus Rift, bringing the dream of immersive virtual experiences to living rooms around the world. Today, the origins of VR serve as a testament to the human desire to push boundaries and explore uncharted territories. What began as a concept rooted in science fiction has evolved into a tangible technology with the power to revolutionize how we work, learn, and entertain ourselves. The journey from Sensorama to modern VR headsets is a testament to human ingenuity and the relentless pursuit of creating a world beyond the confines of reality.

The evolution of Virtual Reality has been nothing short of remarkable. From its humble beginnings as a futuristic concept to the sophisticated technology we have today, VR has matured into a powerful tool with applications that extend far beyond entertainment. In the realm of entertainment and gaming, VR has redefined the user experience. No longer confined to traditional screens, users can now immerse themselves in virtual worlds where they become active participants rather than passive observers. Games like "Beat Saber" and "Half-Life: Alyx" showcase the potential of VR in storytelling, interactivity, and the sheer joy of exploration. Education has undergone a transformation with the integration of VR. Imagine students dissecting virtual organisms or stepping into historical events, making learning a vivid and engaging experience. VR is breaking down the barriers of traditional education, offering a dynamic platform for exploration and discovery. In the medical field, VR is not just a technological marvel; it's a lifesaver. Surgical training, therapy sessions, and pain management are areas where VR is making significant contributions. Companies like Touch Surgery are pioneering the use of VR to enhance surgical skills, ultimately improving patient outcomes. The legal sector, too, has embraced VR. Virtual crime scene recreations, courtroom visualizations, and virtual training for legal professionals are changing the way law is practiced. VR's immersive capabilities are proving invaluable in enhancing understanding and presenting evidence. Tourism has experienced a revolution thanks to VR. Travel enthusiasts can explore destinations virtually, providing a preview that goes beyond traditional brochures. This not only enhances the travel experience but also makes it more accessible to individuals who may face physical or financial constraints. In science and engineering, VR has become an indispensable tool. Scientists can visualize complex data, engineers can design prototypes, and both can simulate experiments in a virtual environment. This not only accelerates the pace of innovation but also opens up new possibilities for discovery.

The present applications of VR illustrate its versatility and potential to redefine the way we experience various aspects of life. From entertainment and education to healthcare and beyond, VR is leaving an indelible mark on our world, laying the foundation for a future where the virtual and the real seamlessly coexist. As the applications of Virtual Reality continue to expand, so too does its impact on the global economy. Beyond its technological marvel, VR has become a catalyst for economic growth, spawning new industries, startups, and job opportunities. The economic ripple effect of VR is evident in the emergence of companies that have become household names. Oculus, founded in 2012 and later acquired by Facebook, exemplifies the success story of a startup that dared to redefine an industry. Oculus Rift, its flagship VR headset, became a game-changer, sparking widespread interest and investment in virtual reality. Startups like Magic Leap have further pushed the boundaries of VR with their mixed reality technology. Beyond the realms of gaming and entertainment, Magic Leap has ventured into healthcare and enterprise solutions, showcasing the diverse applications and potential of VR in shaping industries beyond our imagination.

The growth of the VR industry has not only led to the success of major players but has also created a fertile ground for startups and entrepreneurs. From hardware development to content creation, the VR ecosystem is teeming with opportunities for those willing to innovate and explore uncharted territories.

Moreover, the demand for skilled professionals in the VR space has surged. Roles in VR development, content creation, and user experience design have become sought-after, paving the way for a new generation of technologically savvy individuals. As VR continues to integrate into various sectors, the job market is expected to see a significant influx of positions catering to the growing demand for VR expertise. The economic impact of VR extends beyond job creation. It influences research and development expenditures, fosters innovation, and contributes to a more robust and dynamic economy. The success stories of Oculus and Magic Leap serve as beacons, inspiring entrepreneurs and investors to recognize the immense potential within the virtual realm. As we witness the economic transformation brought about by VR, it becomes clear that this technology is not just about creating virtual worlds but also about building a tangible foundation for economic prosperity and job creation in the real one. The economic impact of VR is not confined to Silicon Valley but resonates globally, shaping industries and economies in ways that were once considered the stuff of dreams. However, VR brings forth a host of legal and ethical considerations that demand careful examination. The immersive nature of VR raises questions about privacy, data security, and potential addiction, accessibility issues, necessitating a thoughtful approach to regulation. In fact these are the opportunities for young minds to dive into to solve possible challenges.

In the Indian context, the transformative power of Virtual Reality holds immense promise. As a nation with diverse challenges and opportunities, India stands at the threshold of a technological renaissance that can redefine education, healthcare, and economic growth.
In a country with a vast and varied education landscape, VR has the potential to revolutionize learning. Imagine students in rural areas exploring historical monuments, conducting virtual science experiments, or engaging in immersive language lessons. VR can bridge the educational divide, providing access to quality learning experiences irrespective of geographical constraints. India's healthcare sector can benefit significantly from VR applications. Remote medical consultations, surgical training through simulations, and mental health therapy in a virtual environment can address challenges posed by geographical distances and resource limitations. VR can democratize healthcare, making it more accessible to a broader population. For a country aspiring to be a global economic powerhouse, the integration of VR can fuel innovation and job creation. Startups in VR development, content creation, and immersive experiences can thrive, contributing to economic growth. The success stories of Oculus

and Magic Leap serve as inspirations for Indian entrepreneurs to explore and capitalize on the vast potential within the VR landscape. India's diverse landscape comes with unique challenges that VR can address creatively. From virtual tourism promoting cultural heritage to VR-based agricultural training for farmers, the applications are limitless. Policymakers and entrepreneurs alike can collaborate to tailor VR solutions that address India's specific needs. VR presents an opportunity for positive change. It's a call to action for the youth, entrepreneurs, and policymakers—a call to explore, innovate, and implement VR for a better India.

BLOCKCHAIN OF TRUST

From Satoshi's Code to Global Impact, How Blockchain Transforms Every Industry Through Transperency

Imagine a world where transactions are not governed by central authorities but rather by a collaborative network of computers, each playing a crucial role in ensuring transparency and security. This is the essence of blockchain—a technology that emerged from the shadows with the release of a whitepaper titled "Bitcoin: A Peer-to-Peer Electronic Cash System" in 2008. In the early 2000s when an entity known as Satoshi Nakamoto introduced the world to a revolutionary concept—blockchain technology. The underlying technology, blockchain, was designed as a solution to the double-spending problem, ensuring that digital assets could not be duplicated or manipulated. This innovation not only disrupted traditional notions of trust and security but laid the groundwork for a decentralized future. The enigmatic figure behind this breakthrough, Satoshi Nakamoto, remains an unknown force, but their creation has become a cornerstone of the digital era.

Blockchain is a decentralized ledger that records transactions across a network of computers, establishing an immutable and transparent record. Each block in the chain contains a timestamp and a reference to the previous block, creating a chronological and unbreakable sequence. In a traditional centralized system, a single authority or intermediary holds and validates transactions. In contrast, blockchain distributes this responsibility across a network of nodes (computers) that collectively maintain the ledger. Each participant in the network has access to the entire history of transactions, creating a transparent and democratic record-keeping system. The term "blockchain" reflects its structure. Transactions are grouped into blocks, and each block is linked to the previous one through a cryptographic hash, forming an unbroken chain. Once a block is added to the chain, it becomes nearly impossible to alter any information within it without changing subsequent blocks—a quality referred to as immutability.

Blockchain employs cryptographic techniques to secure transactions and control the creation of new blocks. Consensus mechanisms ensure that all participants agree on the state of the ledger, even in a decentralized environment. This trustless and decentralized nature of blockchain reduces the reliance on intermediaries, fosters transparency, and introduces new possibilities for innovation across various industries. It began its journey as the underlying technology for Bitcoin, a cryptocurrency challenging the traditional financial landscape. As Bitcoin gained traction, it became clear that blockchain technology held potential far beyond cryptocurrency. Its decentralized nature, coupled with its ability to establish trust without intermediaries, laid the groundwork for innovative applications across diverse industries.

Blockchain's transformative potential quickly caught the attention of visionaries and innovators. Beyond its role in financial transactions, the technology began to find applications that addressed real-world challenges and inefficiencies. One of the groundbreaking applications of blockchain is in the education sector. Blockchain facilitates the creation of secure and verifiable credentials. Academic achievements, degrees, and certifications can be recorded on an immutable ledger, ensuring their authenticity. This not only simplifies credential verification but also fosters trust in educational institutions. In healthcare, blockchain ensures the secure and portable storage of medical records. Patients gain control over their health data, and the decentralized nature of the technology enhances data privacy. This innovation streamlines healthcare processes, improves patient care, and reduces administrative burdens.

Blockchain's impact on the economy extends beyond established industries. The technology has spurred the creation of startups and job opportunities in fields like cryptocurrency exchanges, blockchain development, and decentralized applications (DApps). This economic shift is not just about financial transactions; it's about redefining how we interact with information and value. In the legal domain, smart contracts have emerged as a game-changer. These self-executing contracts, encoded with predefined rules, automate and enforce agreements. This not only reduces the need for intermediaries but also enhances the efficiency of contractual processes. Decentralized dispute resolution mechanisms, powered by blockchain, provide a transparent and efficient alternative to traditional legal frameworks. The tourism industry, often plagued by issues of authenticity and trust, has found a reliable ally in blockchain. From validating the legitimacy of accommodations to authenticating user reviews, blockchain ensures transparency in the travel sector. Travelers can trust that the services they book are genuine, and the reviews they read are unaltered, creating a more reliable and enjoyable travel experience. Governance, a cornerstone of societal functioning, is undergoing a transformation with blockchain technology. Transparent and tamper-proof election systems, powered by blockchain, are being explored and implemented in various regions. This ensures the integrity of democratic processes, offering citizens confidence in the fairness and authenticity of their votes. Implementing blockchain technology for submission, processing and and collection of various documents, could be certainly an handshake between citizens and governments.

In the ever-evolving landscape of technological innovation, Western countries have been at the forefront of embracing blockchain. From the bustling streets of Silicon Valley to government-backed initiatives in Europe, the technology has catalyzed economic growth, transparency, and efficiency. Blockchain has spawned a wave of startups, with Silicon Valley becoming a hub for blockchain development and cryptocurrency innovation. Governments in Europe, recognizing the potential benefits, have initiated blockchain-friendly policies and pilot projects. The result is a symbiotic relationship between technology, innovation, and economic progress. The adoption of blockchain in these regions has not only led to economic transformations but has also positioned them as pioneers in the global digital revolution.

The evolution of blockchain technology brings with it a series of legal and ethical considerations. Striking the right balance between fostering innovation and safeguarding against potential risks is a challenge governments across the globe are grappling with. Governments are working to create regulatory frameworks that encourage innovation while ensuring consumer protection. Issues such as fraud, money laundering, and data privacy require thoughtful consideration and proactive regulatory measures. As the technology matures, collaboration between industry stakeholders, policymakers, and legal experts becomes crucial to establishing a secure and ethical foundation for blockchain's widespread adoption. As with any revolutionary technology, blockchain is not without its challenges. Scalability issues, concerns about energy consumption in certain consensus mechanisms, and the lack of standardized global regulations pose hurdles to its seamless integration into mainstream systems.

However, the future of blockchain appears promising. Technological advancements, ongoing research, and collaborative efforts within the industry are addressing these challenges. In India, a nation with a burgeoning population and diverse challenges, blockchain holds the key to building a more transparent, efficient, and equitable future. By inspiring the youth, entrepreneurs, and policymakers to explore and implement blockchain technology, India can embark on a journey that transcends traditional boundaries, unlocking new possibilities for economic growth, social development, and global collaboration.

SMART AGRICULTURE & FARMING

Transforming Agriculture from need, to impact and future sustainability.

In the tapestry of human history, agriculture has woven the very fabric of our survival. From the earliest days of sowing seeds in fertile soil to the present era of technological marvels, agriculture has undergone a profound metamorphosis. To truly appreciate the current landscape of agriculture, we must cast our gaze back to its humble origins. Millennia ago, our ancestors tilled the land with simple tools, relying on instincts and the rhythm of seasons. Agriculture laid the foundation for settled societies, transforming nomadic wanderers into cultivators of the earth. The knowledge passed down through generations became the bedrock of traditional farming practices, where manual labor, intuition, and an intimate connection to the land dictated the success of a harvest.

The turning point arrived with the agricultural revolution, marking the introduction of machinery and the dawn of mechanized farming. Tractors plowed fields, and combine harvesters reaped crops at an unprecedented pace. However, the true revolution emerged with the integration of smart technologies. Precision agriculture, equipped with GPS and sensors, allowed farmers to treat each field uniquely, optimizing resources. This leap into smart farming introduced a new era where artificial intelligence, Internet of Things (IoT), and automation became the keystones of a technological renaissance in agriculture. In the contemporary agricultural landscape, technology stands as a silent, but powerful, ally to farmers worldwide. Precision farming has evolved, now enabling farmers to deploy sensors, monitor crops in real-time, and optimize irrigation, thereby reducing waste. Artificial Intelligence, the wizard behind the scenes, empowers predictive analytics for disease detection, crop management, and yield optimization. Drones soar above fields, capturing data that guides decision-making, from planting to harvest. These advancements not only enhance efficiency but also contribute to the sustainability of agriculture in the face of modern challenges.

Around the globe, agricultural success stories illustrate the transformative impact of technology. The Netherlands, a pioneer in vertical farming, demonstrates how innovative practices ensure year-round crop production. In the heartland of the United States, large-scale farms utilize automated machinery and data analytics to redefine productivity. Meanwhile, India, with its diverse agricultural landscape, showcases how technology-driven apps connect farmers with market prices, fostering transparency and equitable trade. The marriage of technology and agriculture not only cultivates crops but also sprouts economic opportunities. The rise of agtech startups, specializing in precision farming and sustainable practices, has become a beacon of innovation. These ventures not only create jobs but contribute to economic growth on a global scale. The intertwining of technology and agriculture is not merely a revolution in the fields; it's a burgeoning economic force, fostering entrepreneurship and propelling the sector into uncharted territory.

In the bustling city-state of Singapore, where arable land is scarce, vertical farming has emerged as a game-changer. Cutting-edge hydroponics systems and controlled environments enable the cultivation of crops in stacked layers, maximizing space and resources. This not only ensures a consistent and year-round supply of fresh produce but also minimizes the environmental footprint associated with traditional farming. Brazil, a global agricultural powerhouse, has harnessed the power of artificial intelligence for precise crop prediction. By analyzing vast amounts of data, including climate patterns, soil health, and historical crop performance, AI algorithms provide farmers with accurate forecasts. This not only aids in planning and resource allocation but also enhances overall crop yields, contributing to the country's robust agricultural output. In the quest for food authenticity and ethical sourcing, blockchain technology has found a place in organic farming. Transparent and immutable, blockchain ensures the traceability of organic produce from farm to table. This not only fosters consumer trust but also provides a fair market value for farmers committed to sustainable and organic practices. The vast farmlands of the United States have witnessed a technological renaissance. Automated machinery, equipped with GPS guidance systems, streamlines planting and harvesting processes. Advanced data analytics enable farmers to make data-driven decisions, optimizing resource use and maximizing yields. This not only ensures the nation's food security but also positions it as a global agricultural leader. In the Netherlands, a country with limited arable land, vertical farming has become a symbol of agricultural innovation. Controlled-environment agriculture, leveraging technologies such as hydroponics and aeroponics, allows for year-round production in urban settings. This not only addresses land scarcity issues but also sets an example for sustainable and efficient urban agriculture. Facing the challenges of a harsh climate, Australian farmers have embraced technology to overcome adversity. Precision farming techniques, coupled with sensor technologies, enable farmers to adapt to arid conditions and optimize water usage. Additionally, the use of satellite imagery and drones aids in monitoring vast agricultural landscapes, enhancing overall productivity and sustainability.

As the global population continues its upward trajectory, and climate change disrupts traditional farming practices, technology emerges as a beacon of hope. Precision agriculture, with its data-driven approach, enables farmers to adapt to changing climate conditions. Drones equipped with sensors monitor crop health, detecting diseases and pests early on. Genetic engineering and biotechnology contribute to the development of drought-resistant and high-yield crops, addressing concerns about food scarcity and hunger. Technology's role in mitigating climate change impacts on agriculture is not just about resilience; it's about forging a sustainable path forward. The ability to harness data, analytics, and innovation positions agriculture as a dynamic and responsive industry in the face of global challenges. The synergy between big data and agriculture is a pivotal force in achieving sustainability. By leveraging data analytics, farmers can make informed decisions about crop rotation, optimal planting times, and resource utilization. Drones equipped with multispectral cameras provide real-time insights into crop health, reducing the reliance on chemical interventions and fostering environmentally friendly farming practices.

However, this technological leap is not without its ethical challenges. Questions surrounding data privacy, ownership, and the potential for technology to exacerbate socio-economic divides are pressing concerns. Striking a delicate balance between innovation and ethical responsibility is paramount to ensuring that the benefits of technology are shared equitably, especially among low-income farmers.

The fusion of technology and agriculture is not merely an enhancement of crop yields; it's a catalyst for economic growth on a global scale. The emergence of agtech startups has breathed new life into the agricultural landscape, introducing innovative solutions and fostering entrepreneurship. Technology in agriculture has become a powerful engine for job creation. From skilled technicians managing precision farming equipment to data analysts interpreting vast sets of agricultural data, the sector now demands a diverse range of talents. This not only bolsters rural economies but also attracts a new generation to the fields of science, technology, engineering, and mathematics (STEM). Startups specializing in precision agriculture, sustainable practices, and agri-fintech are injecting fresh ideas into an age-old industry. These ventures not only create jobs but also stimulate local economies and contribute to a more resilient and adaptable agricultural sector. Beyond job creation, the economic impact of technology in agriculture resonates globally. As countries adopt smart farming practices, they become more efficient in food production, contributing to food security. Moreover, the export of agtech solutions, machinery, and expertise becomes a lucrative avenue for economic growth. The symbiosis of technology and agriculture propels nations into the forefront of global trade and innovation. As we stand at the crossroads of tradition and innovation, the positive impact of technology on agriculture paints a promising picture for the future. Beyond the efficiencies gained and economic opportunities created, technology in agriculture is a beacon of hope for sustainability. It empowers farmers to be stewards of the land, utilizing data and innovation to foster practices that are not just productive but also environmentally conscious.

In the Indian context, where agriculture is intertwined with the country's identity, the message is clear: embrace technology for a better tomorrow. By leveraging smart solutions, India can address the challenges of a growing population, ensure food security, and uplift the lives of millions of farmers. The call goes out to the youth, entrepreneurs, and policymakers to explore, innovate, and implement technology in agriculture, paving the way for a resilient and prosperous India.

AI IS AT HUMAN DISPOSAL

Embracing AI for a Better Future, turning Dreams into Reality.

Artificial Intelligence, a phrase once confined to science fiction, has rapidly become an integral part of our reality, influencing every facet of our lives. In the mid-20th century, visionaries like Alan Turing laid the conceptual groundwork for what we now know as Artificial Intelligence. Back then, it was more aspiration than achievement. However, as computing power and machine learning capabilities surged, the dream of machines emulating human intelligence became a tangible reality. The intrigue surrounding AI isn't just about the present or future; it's about understanding how far we've come and appreciating the relentless pursuit of creating machines that can think, learn, and adapt.

The roots of Artificial Intelligence can be traced back to a time when the concept of machines possessing human-like intelligence captured the imaginations of scientists and thinkers. Alan Turing, a pioneering figure in computer science, laid the groundwork with his proposal of the Turing Test in the 1950s. This test, which challenged machines to exhibit intelligent behavior indistinguishable from that of humans, marked the conceptual birth of AI. The journey continued with the development of early AI programs that could perform basic tasks and logical reasoning. However, progress was slow, and optimism waned in what became known as the "AI winter." It wasn't until the resurgence of interest in the 1980s, fueled by advancements in computing power and algorithmic innovations, that AI experienced a renaissance. A breakthrough came with the advent of neural networks, inspired by the human brain's structure. This approach, coupled with the availability of vast datasets, ushered in a new era of machine learning. The rise of AI, which had once seemed like a distant dream, became an accelerating reality.

In the present era, Artificial Intelligence has woven itself into the fabric of our daily lives, seamlessly infiltrating various sectors with groundbreaking innovations. The traditional classroom is undergoing a metamorphosis as AI-powered educational tools cater to individual learning styles. Platforms like Khan Academy leverage machine learning algorithms to personalize lessons, adapting to the unique needs of each student. This not only enhances comprehension but also fosters a more inclusive and dynamic learning environment. Governments worldwide are turning to AI for data-driven decision-making. Analyzing vast datasets allows for more efficient resource allocation, optimized public services, and timely policy adjustments. The integration of AI in governance promises a more responsive and transparent administration. The automotive industry is at the forefront of AI innovation with the development of autonomous vehicles. Companies like Tesla are pushing boundaries, introducing self-driving features that aim to revolutionize transportation. The potential benefits include reduced accidents, increased efficiency, and improved accessibility, especially for individuals with mobility challenges. AI is a game-changer in healthcare, offering solutions to long-standing challenges. Diagnostic tools powered by machine learning can analyze medical images with unparalleled accuracy, aiding in early detection and precise treatment plans. Additionally, predictive analytics contribute to personalized medicine, optimizing patient outcomes. Language is no longer a barrier, thanks to AI-driven language translation services. From real-time translation in conversation to breaking down language barriers in written communication, AI is fostering global connectivity. Voice assistants and chatbots further streamline communication, offering a glimpse into a future where language is effortlessly transcended. AI is transforming the legal landscape, automating labor-intensive tasks such as document analysis and research. Predictive analytics assist legal professionals in predicting case outcomes and formulating effective strategies. The result is increased efficiency, reduced costs, and improved access to legal resources. The intersection of AI and the arts is yielding fascinating results. From algorithm-generated artworks to AI-assisted music composition, machines are challenging traditional notions of creativity. Collaborations between human artists and AI algorithms are pushing the boundaries of what's artistically possible. The vastness of space exploration benefits from AI's ability to process immense datasets. Machine learning algorithms assist in analyzing complex astronomical data, identifying patterns, and uncovering insights that might elude traditional methods. AI is a valuable tool in the quest to unravel the mysteries of the cosmos. AI-driven analytics and automation are reshaping the landscape. From predictive sales forecasting to supply chain optimization, businesses are leveraging AI to gain a competitive edge. Startups and established enterprises alike are embracing AI to drive innovation, enhance customer experiences, and boost overall efficiency.

The impact of Artificial Intelligence extends beyond innovation; it is a powerful catalyst for economic transformation on a global scale. As AI infiltrates industries, it not only redefines business processes but also spawns new job opportunities, fosters the rise of startups, and reshapes the economic landscape. The economic ripple effect begins with the emergence of startups dedicated to AI-driven solutions. Silicon Valley, often considered the epicenter of technological innovation, has witnessed the birth and exponential growth of numerous AI startups. These enterprises, ranging from niche applications to comprehensive AI platforms, contribute to the dynamism and competitiveness of the global market. Furthermore, the demand for skilled AI professionals has skyrocketed, creating a surge in job opportunities. From data scientists and machine learning engineers to AI ethicists and researchers, the job market is witnessing a paradigm shift. This demand for expertise is not limited to tech giants but extends to businesses across diverse sectors looking to harness the potential of AI for growth and efficiency. India, in particular, has emerged as a significant player in the AI talent pool. With a robust IT industry and a burgeoning startup ecosystem, the country is nurturing a new generation of AI experts. Institutes and online platforms offering AI courses are experiencing unprecedented enrollment, reflecting the enthusiasm and recognition of AI as a transformative force.

Beyond its applications in specific sectors, Artificial Intelligence is proving to be a powerful tool in addressing some of the most pressing and fundamental challenges humanity faces. From climate change to resource optimization, AI is at the forefront of finding innovative solutions to complex problems. The essence of AI as a problem solver lies in its ability to process and analyze data at a scale and speed beyond human capacity. By leveraging AI, we are not merely confronting challenges but gaining the tools to proactively address them. This aligns with the fundamental ethos of AI – to augment human capabilities and enable us to tackle complex issues collectively.

The widespread use of AI involves the collection and analysis of vast amounts of data. Ensuring the privacy and security of this data is paramount. Striking the right balance between utilizing data for innovation and protecting individuals' privacy is an ongoing challenge. Rigorous measures, such as robust encryption and transparent data governance, are crucial to address these concerns. As AI systems become increasingly sophisticated, ethical considerations come to the fore. Issues such as bias in algorithms, accountability for decision-making, and the impact on marginalized communities must be carefully addressed. The ethical development and deployment of AI require a collaborative effort from researchers, developers, policymakers, and the public.

While AI enhances efficiency, it's essential to preserve the human touch. The collaborative partnership between humans and AI, often referred to as augmented intelligence, acknowledges that certain tasks are better suited for human intuition and empathy. Striking a balance where AI augments human capabilities without replacing them entirely ensures a harmonious integration of technology into our daily lives. The continual evolution of AI introduces new challenges. Technologies like ChatGPT, Google Bard, Google Gemini, a recent addition to the AI landscape, present exciting possibilities but also raise questions about their societal impact. Ongoing dialogue and transparency in the development of such technologies are critical to addressing concerns and ensuring responsible deployment. The integration of AI into our daily lives has become so seamless that we often interact with intelligent systems without consciously realizing it. From voice-activated assistants like Siri and Alexa to predictive algorithms shaping our online experiences, AI has become a silent companion, influencing how we work, communicate, and navigate the world. The question of whether AI is a friend or foe is nuanced. While it enhances efficiency, convenience, and creativity, it also raises concerns about privacy, influence, and the potential erosion of human agency. Striking a balance involves actively engaging with AI technologies, understanding their capabilities and limitations, and advocating for responsible development and use.

AI by visionaries like Alan Turing to the current landscape of neural networks, predictive analytics, and intelligent systems woven into the fabric of our daily lives, we witness a story of relentless innovation and human ingenuity. The challenges and ethical considerations underscore the responsibility that comes with wielding such a powerful tool. While acknowledging the economic impact, job opportunities, and groundbreaking innovations AI brings, it is crucial to recognize the dual nature of this technological force. AI, at its core, is a reflection of human intention, design, and values. Therefore, the responsibility lies not just with technologists and policymakers but with every individual who interacts with AI in their daily lives. As we stand at the crossroads of an AI-driven future, the choice lies before us — to approach AI with trepidation or to embrace it as a tool for positive transformation. Let us choose the latter, not with blind optimism, but with informed awareness, proactive engagement, and a commitment to shaping AI as a force for good.

In the Indian context, where a burgeoning tech ecosystem and a pool of talented professionals converge, the call to action resonates loudly. The youth, entrepreneurs, and policymakers in India are presented with an opportunity to not only adopt AI but to shape its future trajectory. By fostering a culture of innovation, ethical considerations, and inclusivity, India can emerge as a global leader in responsible AI development and deployment.

EDUCATION FROM KNOWLEDGE TO WISDOM

A Journey through MIT's Smart Education System and the Future of Learning for smart world generation.

The first day at the Massachusetts Institute of Technology (MIT) was an exciting experience for me. It was thousands of kilometers away from home, and my mind was filled with curiosity about many things. While there was eagerness to learn new things, there was also a bit of nervousness in my mind. Indeed, I felt a bit lost in the vast campus of the university. Then, I took out my smartphone from my pocket. The official app of the MIT opened up. In the extensive campus, I realized where I am located, thanks to the app. I also understood where I needed to go. The app provided unique routes and alternatives to reach there, along with the estimated time required.

In the large campus, I found my niche, and I also discovered where I wanted to go. The app even suggested the best routes and options, along with the time it would take to reach there. To start the classes on time, I decided to visit the library a bit early. At the library entrance, the app provided me with the map of the library building, a list of books, and all the information I needed on my smartphone screen. Just ten minutes before the class, I started moving towards it. Sitting in the class, I opened the timetable on my smartphone and quickly checked the information provided by the professors on the computer screens about the course content and assignments. Throughout the hour, the professors had information on every student's progress, understanding of the subject, and how each student managed their study time. This data made it easy for them to assess the students' performance.

The next day, the study group I am a part of and the room where the group meets were informed to me by the app. However, while I was preparing to go to the library using the app, I received a notification that I could borrow books directly from the library through the app. It would take me an additional five minutes to reach the library, but the message from the study group prompted me to change my plan. With the use of smartphones, computers, and wireless networks, scheduling meetings, reserving spaces, managing study time, and organizing study group activities became much more accessible. With the smart education system at MIT, it is easy to analyze the competition and progress in the entire education system, considering various factors like the students' attendance, arrival and departure times, preferences, study pace, likes and dislikes, besides the various programs, events, councils, and lectures held in the university. This comprehensive information contributes to the competitive development of the education system. The use of technology has made my education more efficient and balanced, enhancing my academic and professional life.

This smart education system, especially in international universities, is being implemented successfully. The data of students, their attendance, arrival and departure times, activities, study pace, preferences, and health-related information are analyzed in real-time. In addition to traditional education, technology is providing a platform for contemporary education, making it easy and enjoyable for students to participate in various external activities and partner with others. The continuous development in the technological infrastructure has made the entire university more efficient, secure, vibrant, and conducive to dialogue. Along with that, virtual learning, audio-visual media, online and distance education have made contemporary education accessible and enjoyable. The 'flip-class' teaching method allows teachers to guide students for self-study effectively.

The integration of technology has not only propelled my education forward throughout the year but has also played a crucial role in the overall development of the education system in the university. The various modern buildings in the university have witnessed the integration of technology, making the entire university dynamic, safe, communicative, and efficient. The use of smart education has made contemporary education convenient and enjoyable for students, facilitating their active participation in various partnerships and contemporary educational activities.

"The face of education has been changing due to evolving technology. From traditional paper books to digital educational resources that shine on mobile phones and computer screens, from blackboards to smartboards, the use of resources has become essential and versatile, ranging from local to international levels. It is now possible to provide and receive updated education according to individual preferences, from entering the educational process as a child to becoming a skilled individual in youth.

To enhance the quality of education and raise the bar, utilizing smart classes has become essential. Implementing data-driven interactive and collaborative teaching methods is crucial for understanding individual progress and preferences. This allows every student to have equal opportunities for success. Analyzing factors such as classroom temperature, light intensity, sound clarity, and carbon dioxide levels can contribute to improving the learning environment. Evaluating the performance of students, teachers, educational materials, and the overall academic atmosphere has become easier with smart objectives (goals) for each component.

For teachers, self-improvement based on performance data is achievable. With student performance data available, identifying areas of improvement and selecting the best resources for future studies becomes feasible. Smart education has the potential to create a workforce that is well-prepared for the market and industry demands. The collaboration between technology and the education sector can enhance communication and understanding between educational institutions and industries. The analysis of student, teacher, educational literature, and the academic environment, along with setting smart objectives for each component, has become a simple process.

Taking advantage of skilled individuals prepared through the education process for the job market and industrial sector becomes crucial. The collaboration between technology and the industrial sector through science and research can enhance dialogue and cooperation. It is important to consider education beyond age limitations, especially in the future cities that appeal to children, adults, and seniors according to their preferences. Ensuring a safe and accessible educational system, especially for women, is vital for the future.

Future smart education is not limited to educational institutions but is an integral component of creating smart cities. Examples like the Grass Valley Campus Garden Window in Washington showcase the potential for architectural excellence in the field of urban development. According to the International Institute of Advanced Studies, future education, with its colors, designs, and shapes, will be more attractive. Smart buildings of schools and universities have become symbols of many cities. The aggregation of small, independent pieces of information and their proper analysis can lead to the modernization and improvement of urban management, making it a smart lifestyle. Promoting 'data literacy' through programs that enhance awareness among students about complex urban issues is possible through smart civic education.

While technology and research may be the main components of smart city development, the development is incomplete without the smartness of citizens. Future smart citizens will be shaped through smart education. Therefore, creating a unified vision for smart education from the beginning of the smart city development process is necessary. Local administration support for smart education encourages students from various countries to be attracted to the city on a large scale. Improvements in the city's economy will support social, geographical, and linguistic diversity, lack of basic infrastructure, and a shortage of skilled human resources. Considering these factors, it is imperative to focus on the extensive opportunities in the education sector in the future smart city.

The ongoing revolution in technology and research, while being a significant aspect of smart city development, is incomplete without the smartness of its citizens. The potential impact of smart education on the future of cities is enormous. To fully harness this potential, it is crucial to have a unified vision for smart education from the early stages of smart city development. The integration of technology, research, and smart education can create cities that are not only technologically advanced but also socially inclusive and economically robust.

MAKING CITIZENS SMART

The Crucial Role of Citizen Engagement in Urban Development.

Any city, village, or locality will be considered 'smart' when its residents have access to clean air for breathing, pure water for drinking, clean footpaths for walking, good mobile connectivity, consistent electricity supply, widespread broadband internet, safe roads and housing, excellent education, organized transportation system, ample space for recreational activities, healthcare facilities, entertainment options, and sufficient food supply. In other words, even though technology can contribute significantly, active participation of the citizens is crucial for the success of smart city initiatives. The main objective of smart city initiatives is to elevate the overall quality of life for local residents. Therefore, the active involvement of local citizens is extremely important in the process of smart city development.

Effective waste management, energy and fuel production, renewable energy sources, alternatives to traditional resources, public information through e-governance, strategies for public safety, video crime monitoring, citizen involvement through eyes and ears, smart meters, water conservation and management, efficient public transportation systems, maximum utilization of public infrastructure, smart parking, as well as digital education through telemedicine are various dimensions where technology, along with citizen participation, plays a crucial role in shaping the future. Sometimes it is observed that governments, despite spending a significant amount, may provide some services and facilities for the citizens, but citizens may not always make effective use of them. Therefore, governments worldwide are encouraging the active participation of local citizens as key stakeholders in the smart city development process right from its inception. Because ultimately, a smart city is meant for its citizens. Hence, understanding what they need, what their problems are, and what solutions they expect becomes more important than anything else.

For city development, seeking various information from the people, asking for new ideas, understanding citizens' opinions on crucial issues, seeking feedback, arts projects, photography competitions, design contests, research forums, and councils filling activities—many such initiatives are taking place around the world to encourage public participation. Genuine benefits are derived from active citizen participation. By actively engaging with citizens, public administrations can develop a sense of ownership and responsibility towards public assets. It is essential to explore new ways for comprehensive urban development. Innovative ideas are crucial. Extensive public participation could make all these possible within the available resources of the city. A good example is the city of Seoul in South Korea, where the administration has initiated efforts to gather information about traffic through sensors installed in buildings and on roads. However, despite considerable spending, the results have not been as expected due to the lack of comprehensive information.

They implemented a GPS-based payment system for twenty-five thousand taxis running on the roads, providing real-time information on traffic. Such initiatives demonstrate how citizen participation can play a decisive role in urban development. There are many excellent examples of citizen initiatives globally. The need to explore information from afar is not necessary. In our city of Nashik, the municipal corporation has also implemented several initiatives through citizen participation. From filling potholes, cleaning garbage, registering complaints through mobiles to appreciating public services – citizens have a positive response. Public participation has proven to be beneficial for administration. By actively participating, citizens not only build a sense of ownership but also contribute to the betterment of future developments. For city development, it is necessary to explore new measures for comprehensive urban development. Innovative ideas are crucial. Comprehensive public participation can make all these possible within the city's available resources. Many examples of successful initiatives worldwide showcase the effectiveness of citizen involvement.

More often than not, citizens have the power to achieve much more than what governments can do. If every citizen remains vigilant about public amenities, and if local entrepreneurs also focus on this, it can result in significant commercial opportunities. As a citizen, you can do a lot. Using your mobile, you can report incidents such as potholes, garbage, accident-prone areas, unsafe places, unclean toilets, reckless driving, theft, water leakage, injustice, harassment, corruption, and such issues to the administration. You can also actively participate in public discussions about major developments. In this way, you can provide additional resources to the government, such as extra electricity, land, and water. Citizens can also become partners in various business ventures. By 2050, 75% of the world's population is expected to be urban, making citizen involvement in smart city development processes crucial for the thriving economy. Therefore, citizens should understand that they now have a role to play in the administration. Being responsible is not just the government's job anymore. Isn't it? Essentially, we are an integral part of the system, and now it's time to realize our responsibility towards the administration. As a citizen, you can do a lot. You can hold the government accountable for its actions. Just like giving your vote in elections is not the end but just the beginning, being responsible citizens is not limited to praising the government; it also involves holding them accountable. Therefore, it is essential to understand that our responsibility is now shared with the government. A citizen can contribute to the administration by actively participating in various initiatives. It is high time we understand our role in building a better and responsible administration.

CLOSURE

High(TECH)Way Forward 2.0

Navigating the Frontiers of Smart Technology and Beyond.

But in the field of Smart Technology, there is much to write about. Beyond IoT, crowdsourcing, crowdfunding, high-speed transport, crowdsourced urban planning, UrbanFlow, traffic routing, artificial intelligence, robotics, virtual reality, augmented reality, deep machine learning, blockchain, and much-discussed ChatGPT or Google Jamini on various subjects will have independent chapters in Tech-Way Forward 2.0. Stay tuned for updates. Please share your thoughts at sunilkhandbahale@gmail.com. Thank you!
|| Hari Om Tatsat||

ABOUT THE AUTHOR

Sunil Khandbahale

Sunil Shivaji Khandbahale, an MIT graduate, is well known Indian technology innovator, entrepreneur, and research scholar. He has been recognised globally for creating KHANDBAHALE.COM, is the second language acquisition technology and digital dictionary and translation platform for major Indian languages. SamaySangitt, Kumbathon for Kumbh Mela, Online Dnyaneshwari Radio, Internet  Community Radio Sanskrit Bharati, GodavariAarti.org, and Language Spellcheckers are a few of his famous technologies. He is an author and also a columnist for reputed media.

know more at https://sunilkhandbahale.com/